First paperback edition 1997

A CIP catalogue record for this book is available
from the British Library.
ISBN 0-7136-4773-6

First published 1989 in hardback by A & C Black (Publishers) Ltd, 35 Bedford Row, London WC1R 4JH
© 1989, 1997 A & C Black (Publishers) Ltd

Photographs © 1989, 1997 Fiona Pragoff

Acknowledgements
Illustrations by Alex Ayliffe
Science consultant Dr Bryson Gore

The photographer, authors and publishers would like
to thank the following people whose help and
co-operation made this book possible:
Jonathan, Aubrey, Katie and their parents.
The staff and pupils at St George's School.

Typeset by Spectrum Typesetting, London
Printed in Singapore by Tien Wah Press (Pte.) Ltd

My Mirror

Kay Davies and Wendy Oldfield
Photographs by Fiona Pragoff

A & C Black · London

In my box, how many shiny things
can you see?

My mirror is hard, flat and smooth.

In my mirror,
I can see my face.

4

But if I breathe on my mirror,
my face disappears.

If I look into my mirror,
I can see over my shoulder...

...and right inside
my mouth.

I'm making a butterfly.

Can you see the other half of my butterfly?

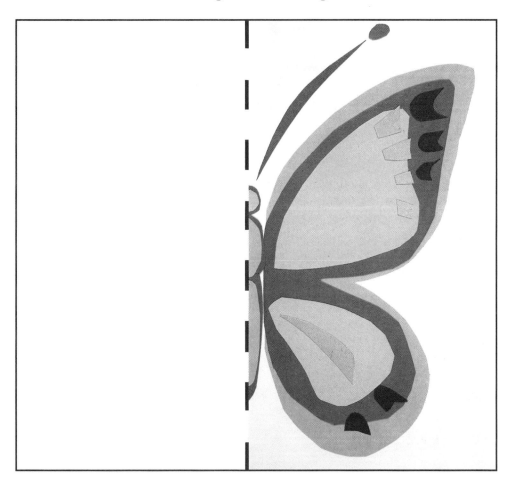

Put your mirror on this dotted line.

With my mirror,
I can bounce
light on to
Andrew's shirt.

With two mirrors, we can see four bricks.

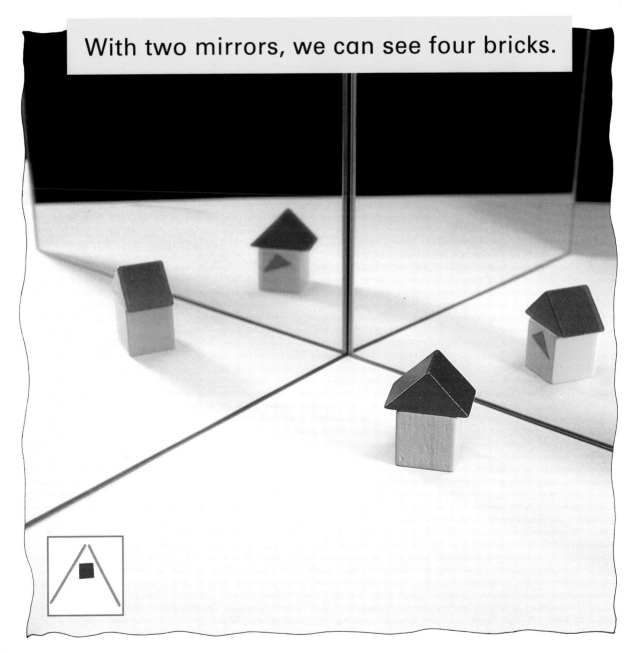

If we bring the mirrors closer together, we can see six bricks.

With three mirrors, we can make a kaleidoscope.

If we drop these paper shapes into our kaleidoscope, what will we see?

16

This is what we can see
down our kaleidoscope.

From underneath, the surface of the water looks like a mirror.

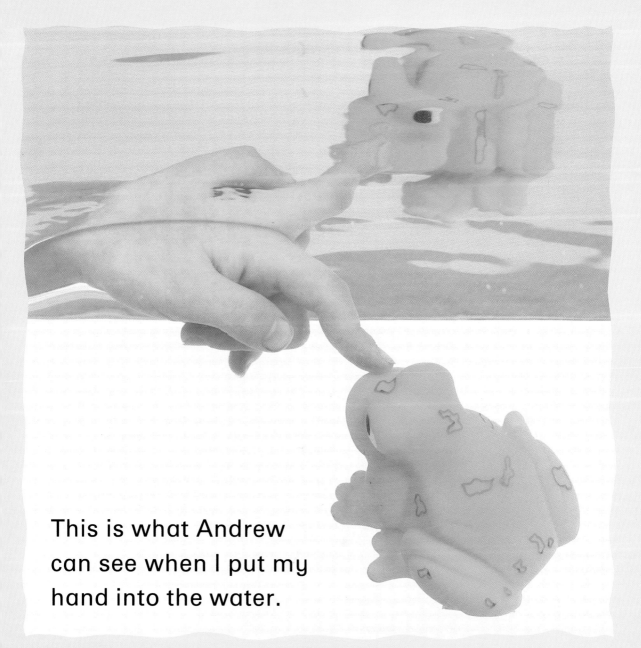

This is what Andrew
can see when I put my
hand into the water.

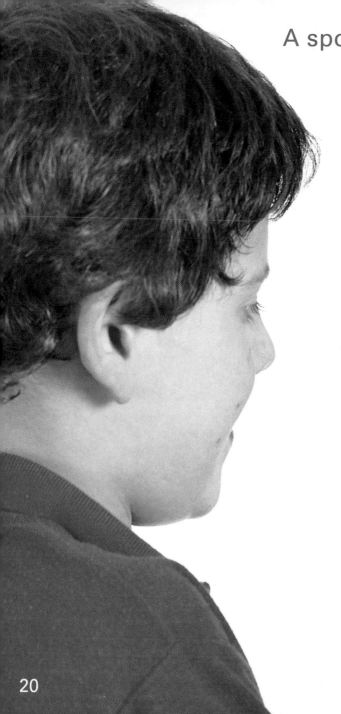

A spoon is like a curved mirror.

In the back of the spoon,
my face looks big and fat.

20

In the front of the spoon,
my face is upside down.

These mirrors
are curved.

They make us look really funny shapes!

More things to do

1. Seeing your reflection
How many different things can you find in which you can see your reflection? What sort of materials are they made of? Are they all smooth and shiny?

2. All sorts of mirrors
How many different mirrors can you find at home, at school or in the shops? What shapes and sizes are they? When you look in a mirror, where does your reflection seem to be? Why do cars have mirrors inside the windscreen and outside the doors?

3. Mirror writing
You can write a secret message in mirror letters. To do this, put a piece of paper in front of a mirror, look in the mirror (not at the paper) and slowly write the letters of your message. When you take away the mirror, you won't be able to read the message. But if a friend puts a mirror next to the paper, they will be able to read the secret letters.

4. Dental mirrors
Next time you visit the dentist, look at the mirror the dentist uses to see all round inside your mouth. What shape is the dentist's mirror?

5. How mirrors are used
See if you can find out how mirrors are used in microscopes, periscopes and telescopes.

Find the page

This list shows you where to find some of the ideas in this book.

Notes for parents and teachers

As you share this book with young children, these notes will help you to explain the scientific concepts behind the different activities.

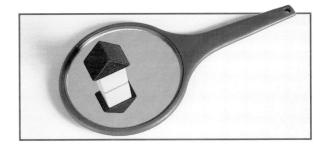

Pages 2, 3 Shiny things
When light hits a surface, it bounces off again. It is reflected from the surface. Smooth, flat, shiny surfaces produce the best reflections. This is why mirrors are made of flat, smooth glass coated on one side with a layer of shiny metal, such as silver or aluminium.

Pages 4, 5, 6, 7 Looking in the mirror
When you look in a mirror, you see a reflection of yourself. The picture of an object in a mirror is called an image. The image appears to be the same distance behind the mirror as the object is in front.

If you breathe on to a mirror, the water vapour in your breath condenses on the cold mirror to form a mist of tiny water droplets. This hides the image.

Pages 8, 9 Mirror pictures
In a mirror, the left-hand side of the object appears to be on the right-hand side of the image and vice versa. Ask a child to touch a mirror with their **right** hand. In their reflection, their **left** hand will appear to touch the mirror.

Some objects are symmetrical. If they are cut in half, one half will be exactly the same size and shape as the other half. A mirror can supply the missing half of a symmetrical object.

Pages 10, 11 Bouncing light
The angle at which light strikes a mirror is equal to the angle at which it is reflected.

Pages 12, 13 Using two mirrors
With two mirrors positioned at an angle to each other, the light can bounce between the mirrors and it's possible to see several images of one object. The smaller the angle, the greater the number of images.

Pages 14, 15, 16, 17 Making a kaleidoscope
To make a kaleidoscope, tape three mirrors together to form a triangle. Put the mirrors on a piece of white paper and drop some paper shapes or beads inside. As with two mirrors, the repeated images are formed by light bouncing to and fro between the mirrors.

Pages 18, 19 Water mirrors
If you look underneath the surface of the water in a tank, the water looks shiny and silvery, like a mirror. This shiny layer reflects any objects which are in the tank.

Pages 20, 21, 22, 23 Curved mirrors
Curved mirrors distort images and change the size of objects reflected in them. Driving mirrors are convex (bulge outwards). They collect light from a wide area to give drivers a good view of the road behind them. A concave mirror (which curves inwards into a 'cave' shape) collects light from distant objects in one spot. Concave mirrors are used in astronomical telescopes to collect light from the stars.

25